Inventions in...

COMMUNICATION

Ian Graham

QED

QED Publishing

First published in the UK in 2008 by
QED Publishing
A Quarto Group Company
226 City Road
London EC1V 2TT

www.qed-publishing.co.uk

A catalogue record for this book is available
from the British Library.

Printed and bound in China

ISBN 978 1 84538 985 7

Author Ian Graham
Consultant Sue Becklake
Editor Amanda Askew
Designer Gaspard de Beauvais
Picture Researcher Maria Joannou
Illustrator Richard Burgess

Publisher Steve Evans
Creative Director Zeta Davies

Picture credits (t=top, b=bottom, l=left, r=right)
Alamy Images David R Frazier Photolibrary, Inc 12b, Greenshoots
Communications 15, The Print Collector 12–13
Amazon.com 5
Apple 23t
Corbis Bettmann 10, 11tl, 21b, Christie's Images 6, Ed Quinn
29t, H Armstrong Roberts 4b, Hulton-Deutsch Collection 22t, Liz
Mangelsdorf/San Francisco Chronicle 22b, Stefano Bianchetti 18,
The Art Archive 7t
E Ink Corporation 9t
Getty Images Fox Photos 4t, Humphrey Spender 14b, Mansell/Time
Life Pictures 20, Science Faction 8
Istockphoto 13t
Logitech 13b
NASA 26, 27
Nokia 2008 29b
Photolibrary 21t
Science Photo Library Geoff Tompkinson 19t, Sheila Terry 17t
Shutterstock 3b, 7b, 9b, 11b, 16, 19b, 20–21, 22–23, 24t, 25,
26–27, 28
Topham Picturepoint World History Archive 17b
Xerox Corporation 11tr

Words in **bold** can be found in
the glossary on page 30.

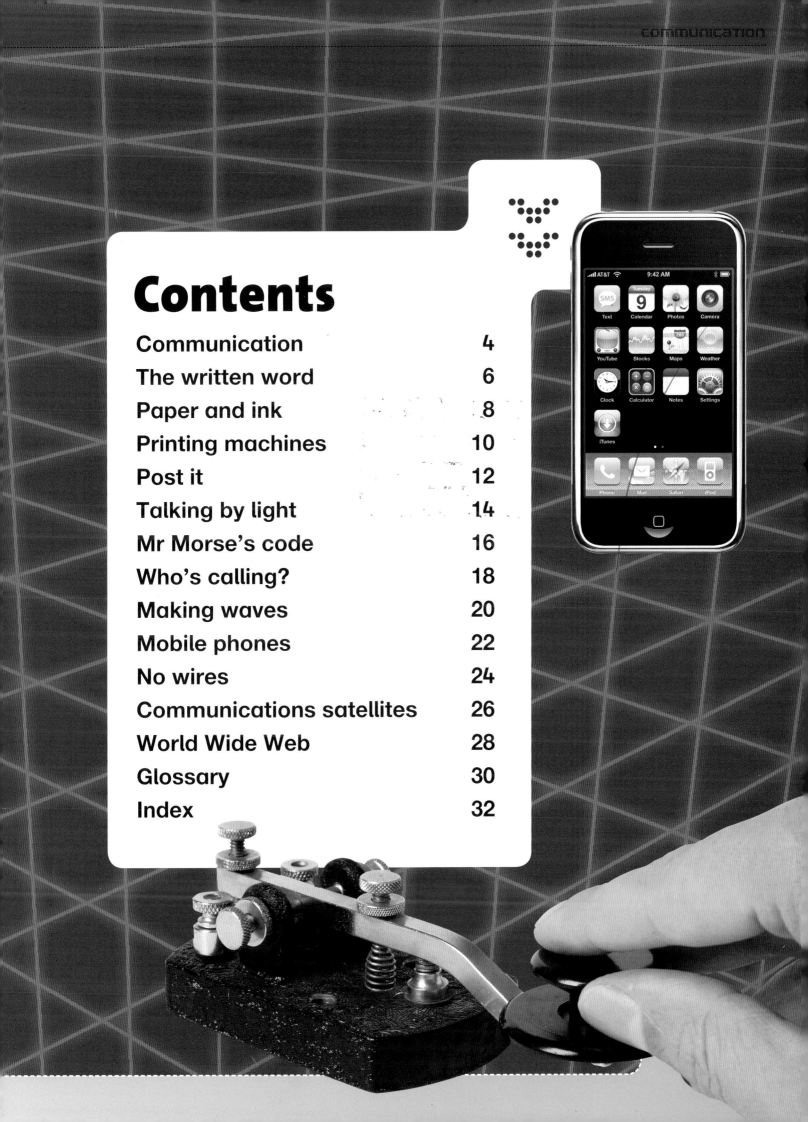

Contents

COMMUNICATION

Communication is the giving and receiving of information. When you talk to someone, you are communicating. Today, there are more ways of communicating than ever before. We can write letters, use a telephone and send emails and SMS.

Reaching further

Until the 1800s, people could only communicate with others that they could see or hear, or send a letter to. The invention of the telephone in 1876 meant that we could talk to someone on the other side of the world just as easily as if they were in the next room. The invention of radio in the 1890s meant that we could communicate with something as far away as a **spacecraft** on another planet.

All police cars have radio communications today. The Detroit police department was the first to fit its cars with radios in 1928.

This early candlestick phone had a separate mouthpiece and earpiece.

Faster and faster

Inventions have made communication faster. Horses could carry a message across the USA in about ten days in 1860. Today, you can give a message to someone just as far away as this by radio, telephone, SMS or email faster than it takes to saddle a horse!

The Amazon Kindle is an electronic book. The pages of books that are **downloaded** into the Kindle appear on its screen.

Who are the inventors?

Until the mid-20th century, one person alone often invented a new way to communicate. Today, communications inventions are more likely to be made by groups of **engineers** working together. Communications equipment is made by big electronics companies. Their engineers get together and agree how the new equipment will work.

COMMUNICATIONS INVENTIONS

2500 BC	Ink
1500 BC	Alphabet
105 AD	Writing paper
c.1040	Movable type
1450	Gutenberg printing press
1565	Pencil
1609	Newspaper
1837	Electric telegraph
1835	Morse code
1840	Postage stamp
1843	Fax machine
1868	Typewriter
1876	Telephone
1894	Radio
1983	The Internet

THE WRITTEN WORD

The most important invention in communication is writing, more than 5000 years ago. People needed to write things down when they started trading goods with each other. Records of what was bought and sold had to be kept.

Egyptian hieroglyphic writing used pictures and shapes instead of letters and words. A kind of picture writing is still used in China and Japan.

Cuneiform writing is made of wedge-shaped marks in clay. It was invented about 4400 years ago.

Writing

The history of writing began in Mesopotamia (modern-day Iraq). About 5500 years ago, the Sumerian people kept records of what they bought and sold by making marks in soft clay tablets. About 3500 years ago, the Phoenician people invented the first alphabet. The letters of the alphabet stood for sounds, not things or ideas. This led to the alphabets used today.

Shorthand

Throughout history, people have invented ways of writing words as fast as they were said. This is called shorthand. Simple lines and marks are used instead of whole letters and words. Marcus Tiro invented a shorthand system in 63 BC for taking down the speeches of the famous Roman politician Cicero. The most widely used shorthand systems were invented by Isaac Pitman in 1837 and John Gregg in 1888.

The Rosetta Stone

When **archaeologists** discover unknown writing from the past, they try to work out what it means. A carved stone called the Rosetta Stone, found in Egypt in 1799, helped them to understand hieroglyphics – the picture writing used in ancient Egypt. The same message was carved on the stone in three different languages. One was written in hieroglyphics. Another was written in Greek, which they understood. This allowed them to work out how to read hieroglyphics.

The Rosetta Stone is now stored in The British Museum, London, England.

Braille is a kind of writing that is read by touching it. As you slide your finger across a page of Braille, bumps in the paper form the letters and words.

Braille

In 1824, Frenchman Louis Braille invented a way of writing that blind people could read. A pattern of raised dots stood for letters and numbers. The bumps were read by feeling them with the fingertips. The Braille system was used in France from 1854 and then spread to other countries.

PAPER AND INK

When people wanted to write things down, they needed something to write with and something to write on. At first, they wrote on clay tablets and wax tablets with a sharp stick. Later, paper, pencils and pens were invented.

Making paper

Archaeologists have found scraps of paper in China that were made as early as 200 BC. Writing paper that we use today was invented a bit later. A man called Cai Lun, who worked at the court of Chinese Emperor He, invented writing paper in AD 105. Cai Lun made his paper from mulberry tree bark, cloth and fishing nets. Modern paper is made from wood and cloth fibres.

Papyrus

Paper-like papyrus was made in ancient Egypt from reeds growing along the Nile River. The tough outside of the reeds was peeled off and kept for weaving baskets and mats. The inside of the reeds was cut into strips. These were laid on a board and pressed flat to form a sheet of papyrus for writing on.

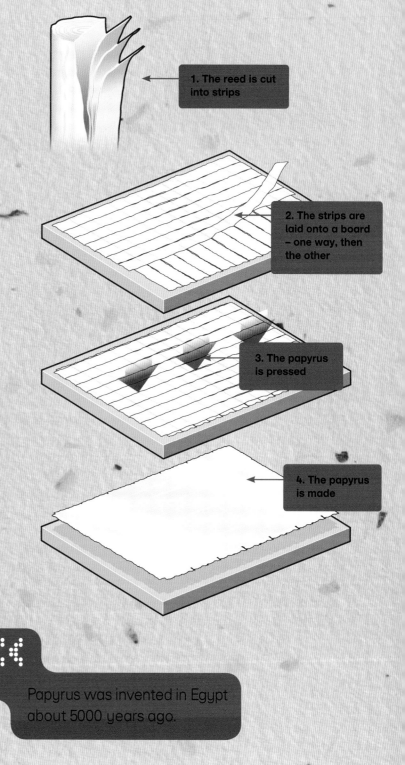

1. The reed is cut into strips

2. The strips are laid onto a board – one way, then the other

3. The papyrus is pressed

4. The papyrus is made

Papyrus was invented in Egypt about 5000 years ago.

The latest type of paper is electronic paper, or e-paper. It's really a paper-thin computer screen covered with spots that can change colour when controlled by a computer.

DID YOU KNOW?

Before people had paper to write on, they used leather and parchment made from animal skins. Parchment is still used for some important documents.

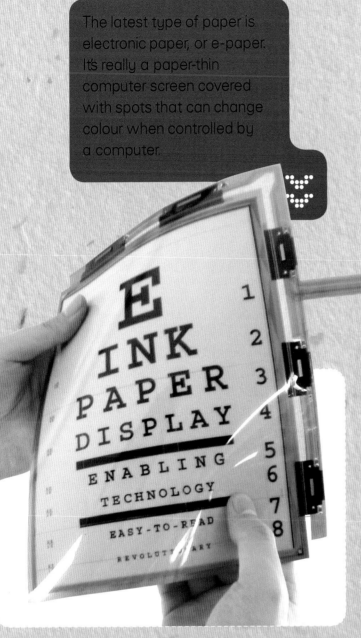

Mixing ink

Ink was invented in ancient Egypt and in China about 4500 years ago. It was made from soot mixed with water and sticky gum. Modern inks are made from more complicated recipes of pigments (colours), oils and other chemicals. They need to flow smoothly, stick to paper and last a long time without fading. Printing inks have extra **chemicals** to make them quick-drying and waterproof.

Pens and pencils

People in the ancient world wrote with pens made from reeds or quills that were sharpened to a point. They had to be dipped in ink after every line or two of writing. Fountain pens, pens with a tube of ink inside, were made from the early 1700s. German-Swiss naturalist Conrad Gesner was the first person to make a pencil in 1565. It was a piece of graphite with a wooden handle. The modern pencil with graphite glued in the middle dates from 1812.

A quill pen was made of a feather from a large bird like a goose.

PRINTING MACHINES

Until the 15th century, most books were produced by copying out each one by hand. This made books very rare and expensive. Then a German jeweller invented a printing press that could produce large numbers of books faster and more cheaply.

The printing press

In 1450, Johannes Gutenberg invented a printing press that used movable type. Movable type is a set of letters made on separate blocks. The blocks could be set in lines to form words. After printing, they could be rearranged to form different words, and used again and again. Before movable type, each page was printed using a block of wood carved specially for that page. It could not be used to print anything else.

Gutenberg shows the first proofs that were printed using movable type.

Moveable type uses letters cast or carved on separate blocks.

DID YOU KNOW?

The positions of the letters on a typewriter keyboard were chosen to slow down fast typists. Typing too fast could make a typewriter's keys jam together. To stop this, the letters used the most often were placed far apart. Called the QWERTY keyboard, it is still used by computer keyboards today.

The typewriter

Printing presses are big, heavy machines. Inventors looked for ways of making small printing machines that one person could use instead of writing everything by hand. American newspaper editor Christopher Latham Sholes invented a small printing machine – the typewriter – in 1868.

At first, the people who used typewriters were called typewriters too. Later, the word typist was invented to describe them.

The photocopier was invented by American scientist and inventor Chester Carlson in 1938.

Computer printers

Lots of different types of printers have been invented to use with computers. The most popular printers used today are **laser** printers and **inkjet** printers. Inkjet printers were introduced by Siemens in the 1950s. The laser printer was invented by Xerox in 1971.

POST IT

People have been sending written messages to each other since writing was invented, but at first only a small number of well-educated, wealthy people were able to do this. Now, anyone can send a letter or package anywhere in the world using postal services.

The first post

Postal services began about 2000 to 2500 years ago, because of the need for kings and governments to collect information and taxes from all over their countries and empires. A postal service called the *cursus publicus* was set up in ancient Rome to carry government and business post.

The Pony Express

In the 1850s, post could take months to travel across the USA. The Pony Express service was set up in 1860 to speed it up. Riders carried the post on horseback, changing horses at stations along the way. They cut the delivery time to ten days or less.

Post is sorted by machines that can read the address codes on letters.

Sticky stamps

The sticky postage stamp was invented in 1840 by British teacher Rowland Hill. Until then, letters in Britain were paid for by the people who received them. The cost depended on how far a letter had travelled. Stamps made mail cheaper, because letters cost as little as a penny to send and there was no charge when they were delivered.

The first postage stamp was black and cost a penny, so it was called the Penny Black.

The Pony Express lasted just over one year until the first telegraph line across the USA was completed.

Post codes

Post codes are letters or numbers added to addresses to make it easier to divide the post into piles according to where it is going. This is called sorting. Post codes were invented in Germany in 1941. Britain started using post codes in 1959, followed by the USA in 1963. In the USA, post codes are called zip codes.

TALKING BY LIGHT

Messages have been sent over long distances by lighting fires or waving burning torches for thousands of years. We still use light for communication today.

Signalling with the Sun

Flashes of bright light can be seen a long way away. Sir Henry Christopher Mance of the British Army made the first device for signalling with flashes of sunlight in 1869. It was called a heliograph.

A heliograph sends messages as flashes of sunlight reflected from a mirror.

A small handheld Aldis lamp flashes messages to a ship.

Signal lamps

Heliographs only worked during the day, when it was sunny. In 1867, British Royal Navy Captain Philip Colomb invented a way of sending messages from ship to ship by light at any time of day or night. A lantern was covered and uncovered quickly to make a series of flashes that could be seen by someone on another ship. A few years later, British inventor Arthur Aldis invented an electric lamp specially for the job. The Aldis lamp was flashed quickly by flicking a lever to open and close shutters at the front.

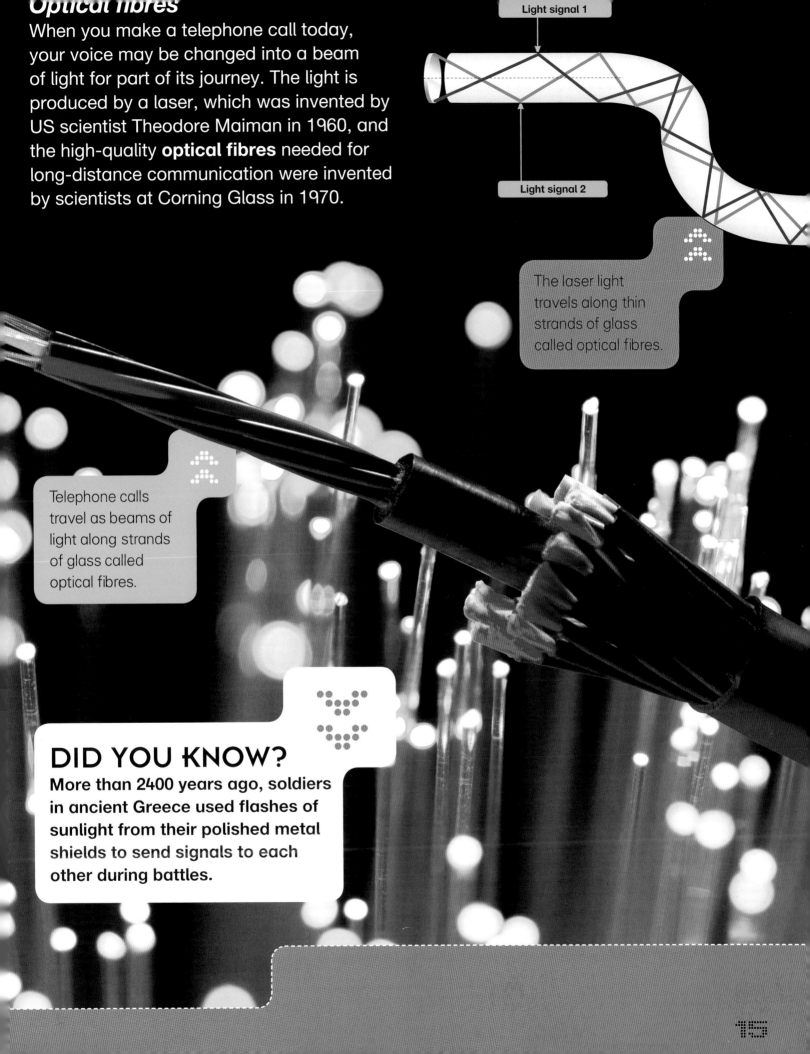

Optical fibres

When you make a telephone call today, your voice may be changed into a beam of light for part of its journey. The light is produced by a laser, which was invented by US scientist Theodore Maiman in 1960, and the high-quality **optical fibres** needed for long-distance communication were invented by scientists at Corning Glass in 1970.

Light signal 1

Light signal 2

The laser light travels along thin strands of glass called optical fibres.

Telephone calls travel as beams of light along strands of glass called optical fibres.

DID YOU KNOW?

More than 2400 years ago, soldiers in ancient Greece used flashes of sunlight from their polished metal shields to send signals to each other during battles.

MR MORSE'S CODE

Modern long-distance communication began with the electric telegraph **in the 1830s. It sent messages in the form of** electric currents **travelling along wires.**

Electric telegraph

In 1831, the US scientist Joseph Henry showed his students an interesting experiment. When he connected a **battery** to a long piece of wire, a bell at the other end of the wire rang. It was a simple electric telegraph. Meanwhile a US painter, Samuel Morse, was trying to build his own electric telegraph. His first attempt in 1835 did not work very well. Then, with the help of US engineer Alfred Vail and information from other inventors, including Joseph Henry, he built a much better telegraph. It was a huge success.

Morse Code

Morse telegraph messages were sent using Morse Code. It was a series of short and long bursts of electric current, called dots and dashes. Every letter and number had its own code. The most famous Morse Code message was dot-dot-dot dash-dash-dash dot-dot-dot. It spelt SOS. It was sent only when someone needed help quickly – when a ship was sinking, for example.

Pushing a morse key down for a moment made a short buzz, or 'dot' Holding down a little longer made a longer buzz, or 'dash'.

Railway signals

The first successful electric telegraph in Britain was built in 1837 by William Cooke and Charles Wheatstone. It worked by sending electric currents down six wires to make needles turn to point at letters. Railways used it to send messages down the line about train services.

Telegraph messages were sent between Britain and other countries by cables under the sea. The first underwater telegraph cable was laid between Britain and France in 1850.

Wireless telegraphy

In 1910, the police in England were searching for Dr Hawley Harvey Crippen, because they thought he might have killed his wife. The Captain of a ship heading for Canada found Crippen on his ship. He sent a telegraph message to the police in England by radio. Police officers raced across the ocean to Canada and were waiting for Crippen when he arrived.

Dr Crippen was the first criminal to be caught with the help of wireless telegraphy.

WHO'S CALLING?

Soon after the invention of the electric telegraph, inventors started looking for a way to send voices along telegraph wires. The breakthrough came in 1876 with Alexander Graham Bell's invention of the telephone.

The first telephone

The first person to make something is not always the person remembered as its inventor. Italian-American inventor Antonio Meucci made a telephone in the 1850s. German inventor Johann Philipp Reis made one in 1860. But Alexander Graham Bell is remembered as the inventor of the telephone in 1876 because Bell's telephone was the first really successful telephone.

Alexander Graham Bell

Alexander Graham Bell (1847–1922) was born in Edinburgh, Scotland. In 1873, he became a professor at Boston University in the USA, where he taught deaf students. His interest in the telegraph and his knowledge of speech and sound led to his invention of the telephone. He went on to produce more inventions, including a metal detector and an iron lung to help people with breathing problems.

Alexander Graham Bell makes the first long-distance telephone call to Chicago, USA, in 1892.

Two hours too late

Every invention has to be made official to stop people claiming they have invented something when they haven't. An invention is made official by applying for a document called a **patent**. The patent says who an invention belongs to. Before anyone is given a patent, they have to prove that they really have invented something new. On 14 February 1876, US inventor Elisha Gray applied for a patent for his invention of the telephone – two hours after Bell!

Automatic dialling

When anyone makes a call, their telephone has to be connected to the telephone they want to talk to. This job used to be done by people called telephone operators in a place called a **telephone exchange**. In 1889, a US funeral director called Almon Strowger was so fed up with bad service from telephone operators that he invented a machine do the job. When a caller dialled a number, Strowger's machine connected the call to the right telephone line.

Telephone calls are connected to the right lines by racks of electronic circuits in telephone exchanges. These electronic circuits replaced the mechanical switches invented by Almon Strowger in 1889.

In 1878, the first telephone exchange was connected to only 21 telephones. Today, four billion telephones are connected worldwide.

MAKING WAVES

We rely on radio waves to receive radio and television programmes. Mobile phones and other wireless gadgets work by radio, too. Radio is vital for communicating with ships, aircraft and spacecraft.

First radio waves

In 1864, the Scottish scientist James Clerk Maxwell thought that it should be possible to make the waves of energy that we call radio waves today. In 1888, German scientist Heinrich Hertz became the first person to make radio waves in his laboratory. He measured their length and their speed, and found that they were the same sort of waves as light, but longer.

Heinrich Hertz was the first person to send and receive radio waves in the 1880s.

DID YOU KNOW?

As soon as Heinrich Hertz found out how to make radio waves and receive them, he did no more work on radio. He stopped because he could not think how these strange invisible waves could possibly be of any use to anyone.

Marconi

Italian inventor Guglielmo Marconi learned about Hertz's work. In 1895, Marconi experimented and built equipment for **transmitting** radio waves. Then he set up companies to do more research and make more advanced radio equipment. Marconi changed radio from something that scientists study into something that is useful for everyone.

Marconi's early radios were used to send telegraph messages. When the passenger liner *Titanic* hit an iceberg in the Atlantic Ocean in 1912, it was one of the first ships to call for help by sending out an SOS.

Broadcasting

Radio signals are **broadcast** by sending them in all directions for everyone to receive. Canadian engineer Reginald Fessenden made the first radio broadcasts from Brant Rock in Massachusetts, USA, in 1906. Telegraph operators on nearby ships were amazed to hear music and people's voices instead of the bleeps of Morse Code they were expecting to hear! Radio programmes were broadcast to the public from the 1920s.

Reginald Fessenden tests the sound broadcasting equipment he invented.